STRANGE PLACES

KATIE GILETTO

STRANGE PLACES

© 2022 by Katie Giletto

All rights reserved. No part of this publication may be reproduced in any form or by any electronic or mechanical means, including information storage and retrieval systems, without permission in writing by the publisher, except by a reviewer who may quote brief passages in a review. For information regarding permission, contact info@courageousheartpress.com.

This book is available at special discounts when purchased in quantity for use as premiums, promotions, fundraisers, or for educational use. For inquiries and details, contact info@courageousheartpress.com.

KatiesPoetryPlanet.buzz

Editing and Cover / Interior Design by
Courageous Heart Press

Illustrations by Charles Vesperman

Library of Congress Control Number: On File

Paperback ISBN: 978-1-950714-23-0

Ebook ISBN: 978-1-950714-24-7

First Printing: October 2022

CONTENTS

A Note to the Reader	vii
Strange Places	1
Probably Bothered	4
Good Grief	6
My Art	9
Speak Out Loud	11
Fruitcake	16
Hunger and Thirst	19
I Hear You	22
Miss Omega	25
The Void	28
Something New	31
Symphony	33
Take Heart	36
Forevermore	39
Pivot	42
Foolish	45
Airplane	47
Limbo	50
The Weather in November	52
Pink	54
Straw Houses	56

Butterflies	58
Weeping Willow	61
The Man of God	62
Chained	64
Three Steps from the Sun	65
On the Fritz	68
Dead Flowers	70
Home Is Where the Heart Is	72
Champion	74
Lost on the Moon	76
Winter Beach	78
The Birth of October	80
Bukowski's Annoying	82
The Starting Line	84
Kids	86
Creepers	87
Big City Dreams	88
Idle Hands	90
S104	92
Red Bumps	95
Rainbow Motion	96
Jelly Brains	98
Rock Bottom Blues	101
Recovery	104

Remember No More	106
Betrayed by the Senses	108
All These Words	110
Man Down	113
No Rest	115
Under My Skin	118
Calypso	121
Whenever You Don't See Me Looking	125
The Lion of Judah	127
The Living, the Liars, and the Lifeless	130
Road to No Place in Particular	132
Thought Flood	136
The Calling	139

A Note to the Reader

I often confuse my left from right. In almost every situation, I'm apt to go the wrong direction. I'm a mess behind the wheel of a car, but I drive anyway. Most of the time, I have to remind myself that just because things are hard doesn't mean I can't do them. Sometimes it's hard to go where you need to. Especially when where you need to go seems unattainable.

This book is about going the wrong direction—and the right one. It's about feeling stuck or lost in the middle of the road, not knowing which way to turn.

We all take turns we wish we could take back. What a waste of time that is. Navigation may only be true when you faithfully follow the blue line on your phone. When rubber hits the road and your options seem to be quickly dwindling, you may jerk your wheel in the wrong direction. I'm here to tell you that it's okay, even if you spin out and end up in a ditch—or in a wilderness you never imagined you would ever be in.

I used to hate hope. I wouldn't allow myself to feel, fearing that hope would leave me disappointed. Fear, an ugly, desperate emotion that is crushing and painful, too often masked itself as the right direction.

Let me share this: Hope will well up in the cracks of the winding and dangerous road you find yourself on. And when you begin to realize that maybe you have a new chance, you run with it because it's all you've got. If you're anything like me, you take a risk and turn in a new direction, even when you fear that hope may lead you further into the wilderness.

The birth of a new direction may lead you far from where you are comfortable. You might end up wandering down paths that your childhood self never imagined you would be taking. Paths that are eerie, shaded, and dark, with poisonous sap oozing from the trees you wish you could lean on. You may find yourself crawling, inching closer and closer to the edge of a high cliff, ready to tell hope to shove it.

Yet this whole time, it's been welling up in the cracks. Look at it. Approach it. Dare to reach for it.

You may wish you had seen it sooner. You long to be where hope tells you that you could be. And that, too, is okay.

A reroute may sprawl out right before you. You may have to double down and start digging to find your path. And as you do, you'll gather courage from the hope in the wounds of the dirt beneath you.

None of us know our left from our right. You will find this to be so in my work. This book has words that will make you ache as well as words that will sooth you.

Don't be afraid of the strange places you find yourself in. Because even there, hope will well up in the cracks.

Strange Places

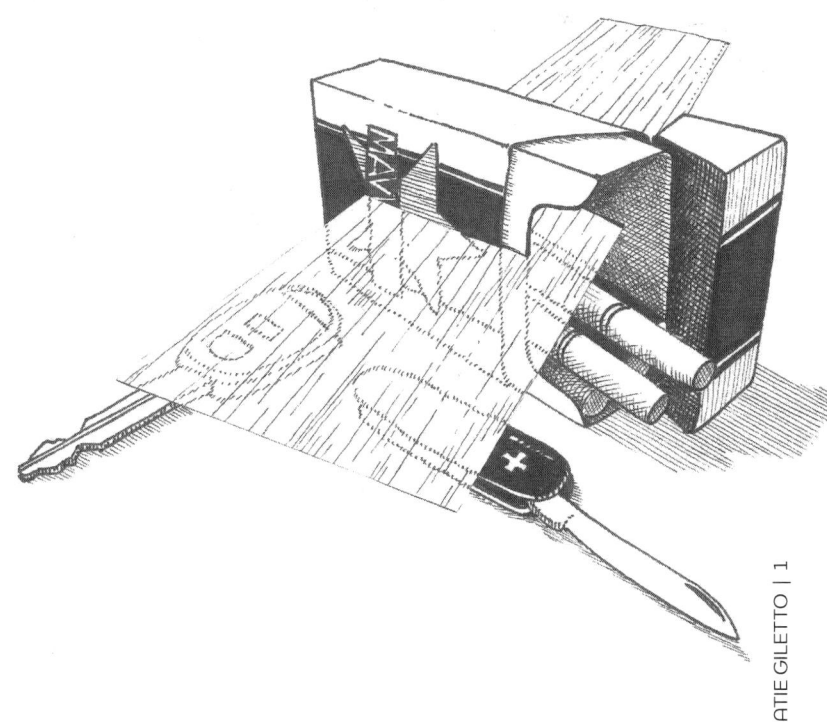

KATIE GILETTO

I pull energy from strange places—
I've fumbled my way into God's good graces
And backflipped into overdrive.

Maybe that's why I thrive in the big city—
When the going gets tough.
I put on something pretty
And push my boundaries.
I revel in making my people proud of me.

I mix my dreams up with reality;
I backslide into a black night;
I bust out my weapon and a flashlight
And sword fight my way into daylight.

Without a prayer,
Feet don't fail me now.
I'll meet you there with my arms out
And dynamite in my backpack.
I'm ready for a sneak attack or an all-out brawl;
I'll take this sprint to a crawl if I have to.
I'll leave hell in shambles when I pass through,
And when bile fills my throat, I'll take a trip to the bathroom.
After that, I'll blend in with the peculiar faces.
I pull my energy from strange places;
I strap on a helmet and double knot my shoelaces;
It's time for some changes.

My dreams descend from the clouds to face reality—
I've got to get these demons out of me.
But I've got work at three,
A couple loads of laundry, and less than $40.
I've got a headache and a stain on my collar;
I've got scars on my legs,
A cluttered bookcase,
And a lamb on the altar.

God, send me a saving grace!
I've got a bad habit of turning my back when I pray.
Somehow, I have a heavy heart with nothing to say.
I pull my energy from the strangest place
And dodge every bullet with a grin on my face.

Probably Bothered

Frustrated probably,
I'm the human anomaly.
I'd disappear, but no one's stopping me.
I could bleed more as they're all watching me,
Irritated probably.
I'm the aborted prodigy—
Watch out if you're crossing me.
I've got a gut-wrenching philosophy.
I'm okay because I've got to be.

I don't have time for your psychology.

I've had plenty of doctors talk to me,
Probably thinking I'm out of my mind,
Yet I know truths that they can't find.
You want to get a rise out of me—
I get it.
You aren't surprising me—

Forget it.
I'm given way too much attention;
I've repented but lack forgiveness.
What a sorry world we live in,
Leaping forward with a grimace,
Sarcastically stupendous,
Good riddance, good riddance,
I'm neither master nor apprentice,

I intended my independence—
But I've fizzled into liquid.
My equipment is faulty,
Lofty heart and stale coffee.
If I disappeared, would you stop me?
If I drain my blood, would you watch me?
I worry not of my body,
But my spirit is splotchy.

Of that I am concerned.
I bet I'll watch the world burn.
Turn the crank, slide the dial,
Let my soul be reconciled.
Do you break, or do you bend?
It's not about that in the end.
Who will ask who played pretend?
I extend my right hand,
But even fiends can do a dance,
Angels sing of a distant land.
If I don't make it,
I'll understand.

Good Grief

I don't speak from spite—
I prefer to turn away.
I have a tendency to be meek
When I feel afraid,
Which is mostly every day.
More than every so often,
I've got a rocket headed toward a comet;
I will rock and roll and prosper on it.
Resting in an open coffin,
I bomb toxicity.
I'm a grenade thrown halfway to simplicity;
I landed in captivity,
Back tracked, and had an epiphany—
Nothing you need to know,
Just anticipate my growth.
I never wanted to be timid,
But I'm stuck in the limits
I built when I was livid.

Now I sit in squalor because I'm so sick of being different.
Yes, woe is me,
But complaining isn't poetry.
Devotedly spirits spoke to me,
Their voices pulling teeth,
Molding broken feet.
They led to my defeat,
Yet it's a comfortable place to be.
All cozied up in towels,
My head splitting open on the couch.
These images that filter out,
They display a visual cacophony.
Whatever it is that you thought of me,
Take it back with an apology.

I may lack in skill,
Though I make up for it in passion.
In my head is TV static.
I'm emphatic in true denim fashion.
Somehow, the holes in my jeans
Lead back to my madness.
They were put there by me
From years of ignoring my own needs.
Again, I say I'm meek.
Damn, there's so much no one sees.
Every day, I buck up,
Put my front up,
Pray for good luck,
Cross my heart and shut up,
My forehead still scuffed up
From running straight at a brick wall.
I got ticked off,
A little bitter and pissed off from being ripped off.

I don't know how I'll pull this off,
But I got a rocket—
Let's lift off.

Fast ball,
My feet slap happy on the asphalt.
I don't run fast, but I'll still turn back to grab, y'all.
After all, I am meek—
Butane turned to poetry.
Strangers don't think the most of me,
But those who know me
Know I will return,
My rocket diving back to Earth,
Not out of spite
But out of motivation to do things right.
My life is not my own;
My actions reflect the ones of those
Who taught me—
Every book, every stern look
That goaded me out of my folly.
The seeds planted took root and are now blossoming.
Whatever it is you thought of me,
Take it back with an apology
Because my heart throbs with honesty.
Honestly, I may be meek,
But good grief,
It's not how I'm meant to be.

My Art

Written in attention,
Scribble in the description,
Lyrical apprehension—
If it's mentioned,
It's crucial.
I don't ask for approval.

If you find my art brutal,
Just know it's my fuel and my fire—
It's my nerve on the wire.
When I know the stakes are dire,
It's my constant reminder
That to inspire is my dream
When my demons come for me.

My art is motivating me,
Lyrical apprehension.
I can feel the mental tension.
It's as if there's friction within,
A cut-throat vision I'm in,
One where decisions are presented—
Scribble in the description.
There is nothing more to me
Than my outlandish, damaged, and candid volitions.
They often contradict my intuition,
My ambition sweating in salty streaks down my temples.
I believe the struggle's beneficial—

Find me somewhere in the middle,
Caught between being swindled and belittled.
Written in attention—
They say one can hear and not listen.
I suppose that's my main affliction.
I feel my neck stiffen
When I'm given instructions,
Learning that there will be repercussions
To my maniacal assumptions,
But there is no pause button
On my constant confusion.

Intrusions and delusions,
All caged away in bruises;
Skipped meals
And to-do lists,
Yet my focus is ruthless.
In fact, it's a nuisance.
When I control the wheel,
I yield no excuses.
I don't believe in "stupid"—
I've seen a mind or two in ruins,
Usually due to my contributions.
I digress; there are solutions.

In art, there are no losses;
It's remedy for your conscience.
Creativity is honest,
Vulnerability softens
The human condition.
Choose your own description—
Peel back the layers of apprehension.
If it's mentioned,
It was written in attention.

Speak Out Loud

I am a poet.

I wish I could do more.
All I have to offer are the words
I scrape off of my hardwood floors,
The words entangled in the laundry
Scattered on my comforter,
Belonging to the roots in the Earth
In the empty pizza box
Or underneath the coffee table.
Unscripted;
Relive it;
Prose written
In padlocks I cradle in my arms.

Slapping snooze on the alarms
That I wound stiffly,
Sickly tearing apart that empty pizza box,
As if the greasy cardboard could let go of

A melodic part psychotic anecdote.
Sell your speech—
If you have something to say,
Don't say it for free.
Deal a fee for your conquest of being heard—
Do not forget your terms
That sparked your mission.
Ask for your settlement in attention
And insist that they listen.
Only once you've happened upon true fruition.

I peel expression from the
Crusted bark of the woods,
And if I could,
I'd render my turn of phrase
For the sake of the good.
My true mistake
Was wandering during developmental change.
Yes, the shift seems out of range.

You too will be mistaken.
You too will be forsaken.
Walk across this lonely planet;
Poet, you won't be abandoned.
Ignore the beasts and grit your teeth—
If you can stand it.
Take root in panic and guard your heart.
Yes, you command it.

Rid me of padlocks—
Let them fall from my arms.
I see you're in shock.
You never knew secrets were like scars,
More than you can count,

KATIE GILETTO | 13

And reluctantly bleeding despite
The frightening midnight.
I'm thriving;
Rewriting;
And underlining,
All the words that slip out from the silver lining.

Yet the timing is off.
What of this earth could I make raw?
How could this tale be so tall?
I see how you're receding—
Take flight and fight as you're leaving,

For if you turn your back,
You will never see me.
Vanished into numbers,
Certainty can be harmful.
I'm partial to fortuity,
So I rest in the den of ambiguity.
It's where I find myself exclusively human;
I'm the kind of warped and whipped lucid.

It's not exactly changing.
Stand back because I'm invading.
I have art worth saying.

Eliminating all the doubt,
You will speak fruitfully among the clouds.
If you want to sing, you can't look down.

I am a poet:

All I have are words.
It's not in your comfort to learn
It brings opportunities for insecurities.

Poet, there is no cure;
There is no congruence or consistency.
Once I've aged, I'll have prayed to see

You chiseling at words that have remained to be discovered
And directed and tended to.

Your people have protected you.
Let your honor be the death of you.

Poet,
If you want to sing, you can't look down.

Poet,
If you want to be free, you must speak out loud.

FRUITCAKE

I am a poet.
I wish I could play sports.
I've turned completely inside out, and no doubt I've pissed off a lot of beautiful women.
I always look both ways but still managed to make a lot of bad decisions,
and in the morning when it's too cold to escape the sheets, I still think about those nights where I shouted from rooftops about women's rights
and the days I spent alone in the woods reading contemporary philosophy because my thoughts
always managed to scream louder than my voice could comprehend.
My shoulders are weak, but my body still demands my mind to speak, but
I could never speak religion, only live it. I could never condone destruction,
just allow constant interruptions to poetic yet manic eruptions.

Is there really much of a difference?
Once I left my sidewalk,
I left my arrows on the ground.
I no longer aim for something beautiful; I do not hunt for angels with cheap glitter.
I follow only my own feet.
I am not afraid.
I have sat under lights outside gas stations,
far past 11:00 p.m., driven by a gust of wind,
watching truck drivers indulge in lust and wink at lost young women,
with dip beefing up half of their lip.
I hear myself ask if this is what we taste like
When we kiss each other.

Can a lover taste those lost nights?
Can a lover breathe women's rights and philosophy?

Do we speak religion as one being?
Can we interrupt destruction with passionate assumptions about nothing but religion,
no matter how many bad decisions or the weight of pleading with persistence?

Is there really?
That much?
Of a difference?

Cigarettes will always smell louder than my voice,
and every thought I carry out will always be tamed by the way my hair sheepishly swings over my face.
Every poem written will be hands on prison walls,
doodles on toilet paper dispensers in bathroom stalls and stuck to my disappearing hubcaps,

and those mornings when it's too cold to move will keep coming until the memories of past lovers and bad decisions and unwanted emotional tension get heaped into one measly load of laundry.
I am a mess in every language.
Pieces of me are scattered all over this dramatically glorified country.
I admit to being a criminal, but I am intentional and handsomely gentle.
If ever I steal, it is only the essentials.
I know I'm making excuses for my embarrassing losing streak,
but if my eyes are windows, then through them, my heart will speak, and the surrounding smoke, cologne, wet socks, and dogs can smell louder than my voice, and I do not have to worry, for I am not afraid.
I am a poet with a closed mouth,
a coward in a doghouse,
an admirer of beautiful women,
a Christian in my intentions but a fool when I make decisions.
Is there really that much of a difference?

Hunger and Thirst

Hold your breath until the lights go out.
Death feels right when the night is out.
Violet windows give
A slight sight
And an ambient sound,
Aroused from slumber
When you saw its glass pound.

Your reason and passion divorced each other
As frigid winds whipped hard even in mid-summer—
Classic love that has grown over one another
With tracks of fatal scars shamefully covered.

You assumed that a train of thought is elastic.
When you pulled too hard,
Reason shot from passion apart,
Like an arrow in the dark,
Yet an arrow of vanity,
No sense of a fleshy ending or strike against humanity,
Just eternally existing in the throes of time and space—
The toothy grin you can't escape.

We scarcely mourned the absence of reason
Because passion took reign over every decision,

How it rants like a tyrant that protects the young.
How does it conquer the lion
Yet drink its blood?

Passion's a villain;
Passion's a dove,
Romantic yet completely abrupt.
Passion is the deep end when you've dropped the bluff
And the lights go out,

All of the depth in the violet glass
Suddenly drought,

Then reason springs out.
Reason is harsh and unattractive,
No better than passion.
Despite its tricks of distraction,
Passion guides us where logic hasn't,
Yet reason calms the rage in love,
Toting the line of clarity and enigmas,
Replacing internal stigmas with radical acceptance.
Reason rules in a father's protection,
It's ever present in a mother's affection.
Betwixt the two, there's no selection.

The daylight speaks loud,
With mighty authority,
Accordingly midnight howls,
Distortedly.
Moral enemies are passion and reason,
Hot coals versus life goals

That change with the seasons.
Strangely enough, the two conquer in cohesion.

The violet window is vibrant;
Passion is such . . .
Daylight is pliant;
Reason is quiet not silent,
Yet there are hearts it can't touch.

Passion without reason is a volatile attack.
The latter can exist alone,
Although its reach cannot atone the weak
Or give solace to quivering bones—
Their reunion is not pleasant but necessary.
I ask you warily craft who you
Prepare to be,
Yet do not plummet into what you're scared to be.

Death may feel right in the absence of light.
Holding your breath as your chest gets tight,
May your window deliver transparent sight
And practical sound,
Yet rarely does clarity freely abound.

Remember the toothy grin you must escape,
The one moving through time and space?
It's the indifference that grows in the absence
Of reason,
Or passion.
There is no choice;
There is no fraction;
Satisfaction may never be reached
Until you learn to balance these.

I Hear You

I've never been any good for anybody—
I've always been too intense.
I've always cared more about my comfort than
My inherently good intentions.

———

This is all wrong;
You know better.
The night is long,
Yet you're no quitter.
Katie, this is only making you bitter.
Channel that energy into something bigger,
Something that holds more power than yourself.
Turn your eyes to me,
Not the tricks of hell.
Child, don't sin;
Child, cross back over the bridge;
Child, wiggle up the towering fence.

The journey is a challenge, but you are a child of might—
You are a child of indignant strength,
Even when you need a break.
In fact, you labor so hard just to hold your mind straight.

Katie, I did not make you to behave this way.
Please don't damage the body I made.
The cuts across your leg
Are a sorry display of who you have come to be.

Katie, I know you know me—
Child, I know you hold me—
Close to your heart.
When you're lonely,
You need to call on me,
Not the blade in your sink.

Do you understand?
There is scripture engraved in your hands.
I have plans;
I have work for you to do.
Don't let the devil make you a fool.

―――

I'm sorry, Father, I think low of myself;
I'm sorry, Lord, I've sinned;
I'm sorry, Father, I feel so helpless,
Yet I know you're the Redeemer—
You rescue the restless.

Don't let me displease you—
Help me do the righteous thing.
Don't let me be a slave to evil—

Let the Savior's blood be my peace.

Miss Omega

The brim
it ripples
it sizzles
there's sparks
it's like a kettle's whistle
the cup begins to dribble
your brain fizzles
then it goes
dark
———

lights on
the kettle is gone

in fact it's somewhere in the Amazon debris
scattered across the kitchen and the front lawn

scraps of metal
shards of glass

the first will be last
yeah? how does that add up?
you'll find out when you spill your cup
boil up let the pot overflow
deserting your own needs
you stunt your own growth
over and over
the last in charge
Miss Omega, you've made your bed behind bars
believe me I see you seething
breathing through your teeth
repeating to yourself

the same clichés for your own good health
well now it's too late
you've bubbled over
talk about making a molehill into a supernova

you rub your own shoulders yet still offer warmth when your own skin is colder

———

Eruption—
Coping by concussions,
The ones you get when
You slam your head with your fist.
Discussions—
Don't fix the tension in your body
When you no longer wish to exist,
All credit to the zip of your lips,
Keeping your mouth shut while you tighten your grip
On the little bit of control you have,
You say you don't get mad—

You pride yourself on that—
Yet, Miss Omega,
Rage has so slowly engulfed your laugh.
It's clouding your path to peace.
I know you can't release
The fury so deep it even spills from your blood.
Grab a mop and some suds—
Rectify the mess you've made in your life,
Slap a hand on the counter to help you get up,
Tidy the kitchen,
And grab a new cup.

THE VOID

Klonopin Remeron,
Clonidine Ambien,
Propped up like a mannequin.
I guess we'll try this again.
They put down my adrenaline;
I don't see the benefit.

Zombie eyes,
I'm alive,
But it's far from paradise.
Psychotically demonetize
All the things I used to like.
Psychosis like a parasite,
I always analyze
The headlights right behind me.
Do you think that they will find me?
Black sedans,
They have an army—
I can't let them recognize me.

Olanzapine,
Mirtazapine,
Waiting room
Magazines,
Office staff so packed
They slide the window,
Slide it back—

Slide the window,
Now you're trapped.

Pissed off, in panic,
Hypomanic and frantic,
Head spinning like it's the planet.

Titanic mode, I'm tyrannical.
Having hope seems hysterical.
By 2 a.m., it's unbearable.
Hospitals are terrible;
You do not get a manual.

It's the gay and the homeless,
The racy mothers, the broken—
Tracks in their toes, it goes unspoken
That you ruin your youth in a moment.
You could call in toxic,
Inpatient,
You're
Locked in,
They let you out in your coffin.
Body safe,
But your brain so drained that it's crawling.
Your friends and family are stalling
To ask their questions.
I'm foggy.
How do I tell them all I'm desperately falling,
Into this shit I keep calling

The void?

So paranoid,
I hear all the noise—
It's more than annoyed.
It's the abyss.
Do you think like this?
Do your eyes display the vapid taste?
The lack of flavor in your face.
Are you afraid?
Do you have a choice?
It's the void.

Something New

**You say you're empty,
but I don't believe you.**
You smile sweetly yet bite the hand that feeds you.
You're ready to leave, but there are people that need you.

You need help,
And I get it—that's scary as hell.
Things will get better,
But only time will tell.

I know you want to do this your way;
You aren't seeing the truth in these clichés.
Every day there are moments that test you,
Thoughts that harm you and rest that will bless you.
Take a second to imagine the best you.
Though you aren't there yet that doesn't make it any less true.

You may think I don't understand
The pain in each breath,
The weight in your hands.
I've felt it—I've lived it; there's no hope in what you've planned,
But I will help you find the strength to stand,
The strength to rise up.
You may think you're weak, but you've done so much.
You have to say when enough is enough.
I'll cheer you on; I'll help you along,
But you're the one that needs to be strong.

I'm not asking you to act like nothing's wrong, like your
Burdens are gone.
I'm asking you to take this day by day,
Minute by minute if you must.
I'm asking you to trust yourself;
I'm asking you to ask for help.

SYMPHONY

I often taste blood,
Like a penny under my tongue.
I sometimes cry when I'm alone.

I'm well on my way to becoming bitter,
Yet I stretch my devotion because God is bigger
Than the figures that pulse in my vision,
Then they wither away.

They erode;
I unfold while He composes.
This symphony is His main focus.

He lifts me to great heights.
I stumble and fumble around like a fool,
And when vipers bite,
He is the one who brings me renewal.

These figures, these strangers, these creepers,
The ones who watch and linger,
Yet His grip is deeper,
His almighty touch.
There's no foe out there
That can snatch me from the palm of God.

Like a penny under my tongue,
I taste the blood, but how much?
Not enough to compare to that day at Golgotha,
When the depths of the devil's breath ran hot with lava.
The sacrifice made on that day
Doused him so deep within because now
The world was saved from sin.

On a rare few days,
I allow myself to wail with rage.
It tastes like blood; it tastes like hate.
For some reason, pain lengthens its stay in my brain.
If the Lord's power can calm the waves
And the storm and noises amidst,
Then he can calm the voices within,

For He has said, and it is written:
Do not be afraid.
The Father instructs us:
Do not be timid.
We are forgiven;
The debt was paid.

I am not bitter nor does fear thrive in me,
And the penny that is tucked beneath my tongue
Serves as my reminder for the living God.
The attack on my mind may be the thorn in my side.
If it persists throughout my lifetime,
I will still rejoice.

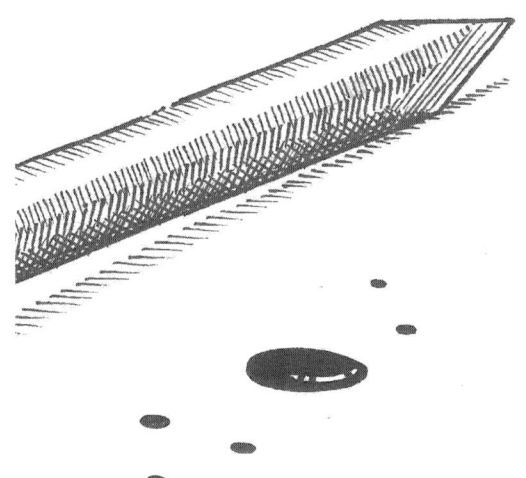

Of all the chaos in me, there is only one voice—
One way—
The only whisper worth listening.
It's the Lord, my God,
Composing my symphony.

Take Heart

Toxic tossed and tragic
you thought this was magic
head buzzing like TV static

paranoid plastered
picking out the pretty things
jewels and gems and gold
where did your promise ring go
spiritual poverty
you're wasting your odyssey
by making a mockery
of a most powerful prophecy
jewels and gems and gold
you're not listening
the scales on your eyes
are morbidly menacing
your shining and shimmering
offers to the enemy are lies

and obscenities of the person
you pretend to be
don't you want to know your true identity

carefully and wonderfully made
imagery painted by the inspiration of the Creator's face
no one can tell the potter what to do with his clay
there are no mistakes

there's no truth in what you think you deserve
the nerve
the entitlement
the price of your life was pure righteousness
accept the word
abandon your idleness

don't think me a prophet
don't think me a saint
don't think me pretentious or pious or fake
I'm rock-bottom material on display
I wear my testimony like a sword and a chest plate
my skeleton is dull but my soul radiates
love rose and doted
passion so potent
that it resurrected the dead and pardoned the broken
the ultimate token of eternity
I can say with certainty
that Christ lived perfectly

don't say no thank you to the cross
take your shoes off
you're standing on holy ground
let that toxicity dribble until it runs out
you may think you're down for the count

when that doubt seeps in
but take heart your faith will bounce you back again

Take heart, there is no greater love;
Take heart, you don't have to be enough;
Take heart, because the God above that we worship with zeal,
The God above that feels what we feel,
That God above will heal when you kneel.

So fall to your knees
And ask Him to cure your unbelief.
Take heart, for Our God speaks in a whisper
With a gentle touch
That we will never be worthy of.
Take heart, because He chose to sacrifice His only Son.
Take heart, for we are saved by His eternal love.

Forever More

If you love me, then stay,
If you don't,
Go away.

That's how it works.
Instead you made promises before you were sure,
Gained my trust, which isn't an easy feat.
I melted to glitter beneath your body heat.

The beat of drums pounding in my chest,
You draw me toward the lion's den,
Yet you backed out when you found I was a Pegasus.

My wings in obvious disarray from the thorns,
You began to pluck them out,
But there were always more.
The horn on my forehead and my habitual doubt,
Stabbing through your melancholy core.

I keep kicking myself for asking for more.
And what for?
I took something I loved and sabotaged it.
No matter how hard I fought it,
I got so close to the eruption I went beyond it.

I used to think your honesty was harmless.
My red eyes say otherwise.
It's foolish, but I always believed in what you promised.

After you leave,
I'll pray to God to conceal the darkness.
Take the poet's words as a token,
Forevermore,
My heart is yours.
All the love I poured
Splattered across the kitchen floor,

The way you looked at me any given moment.
I never thought our love would be homeless,
But the lion has spoken,
His mane curling around his head and face.
The Pegasus broken,
Her snowy fur coated
In soot and smoke,
Yet she knows it was her who
Let her insecurities break bones.

Love me or don't—
You can go.
I've been alone before,
Although this would be my greatest loss.
My love is forevermore.
If I fought,

You'd be gone even quicker.
If I could change it,
I wouldn't have been so bitter.

Just get some sleep;
Have good dreams.
The love in me will grow even bigger.
You probably don't know what I mean—
Go figure.

I don't know what I'm still here for.
Forlorn,
I sit alone in the place of forevermore.

Pivot

Apathy.
It's out of ignorance.
Indifference.
It's escapable if you listen.
We only get one mouth;
It should be used for unity.
Two ears,
So that we may hear
With compassion.

What happened?
Who exactly is floundering and thrashing?
Pity parties and shitty stories are boring,
Yet seem everlasting.

Corpses lie flat in the ground.
The souls are doing the passing.
As they wisp on to great heights or humble loss,

You're still unhappy?
I think I'm getting it.
We're all living with entitlement.
As if we deserve anything more than a pestilence
Of fire and damnation for our
Unholy desires.
Walking on wires,
Trying to do the right thing.
But we are sinners,
So the way of the flesh is enticing.

Apathy.
From a whole generation,
It's nasty.
Indifference,
Demons are laughing.
It's not enough to save yourself,
I'm talking to you, God's people,
Don't turn a blind eye while the devil's lies
Are twisted up in your steeple.

I tell you this:
There will be alcoholics in heaven.
Dahmer had a death sentence,
And he repented.

Apathy.
Indifference.
Every knee will bow
Before God's mere existence.

The power of His hand behind the devil's demolition.
Do you think that some way you'll have a say in it?

Apathy.
Indifference.
We have a role to play in God's mission.
Love, serve, spread the word, with no inhibitions.
His vision is our repentance.
The holy return of lost innocence.
Despite worldly afflictions, we live with intention.
And God's forgiveness has no limit.
Don't go on sinning (of course we will)
But watch how you're living,
For his fingers could collapse our whole world,
Yet we don't live for this earth—it is temporary.
The Prince we serve died to carry
our sin on his back.
Do be wary.
But never hesitate upon reuniting with God's sanctuary.
Unity, one mouth.
Two ears, hear me out.
Let your corpse rot in the ground.

There's nothing left here for you:
God adores you,
the devil scorns you,
angels implore you,
let go of the apathy
let go of indifference
pick up tenacity
uphold your discipline.

Take hold of the Lord in the moment you are living in,
never forget the Father's omnipotence. Come rushing home,
it's not far to go, two ears, one mouth, listen now, just pivot.
It will be your greatest decision in your existence.

Foolish

It was never my duty to save anyone.
I am no healer.
I don't do magic.
I'm a warrior that survived an internal massacre
Between secular hypnosis and
Disasters of divine intervention
I admit: it took a rock bottom or two
To get my attention.
Between relapses, bad habits, psychosis, withdrawals,
Door closes, another opens, and again I choose to fall.
I'm a fool.

My hands are soft despite my ambition.
I have not had to climb as high as others,
Yet this whole time my thoughts are cluttered,
So I'm dedicated to the mission of solving
The tragedy of the human condition that thrives in all of us.
Are we the ones who have labored enough?

I think not—
Not until my hands have grown calloused and worn.
I am far too youthful to be forlorn.

Therefore,
I seek connection,
Genuine infection of the mind.
Could I avoid the trauma and bad karma?
The guilt-driven question of why?

Rock bottom blues had to happen.
My tender hands have never known magic.
My survival was contingent upon those divine interventions,
The sickness that rots my teeth from the bittersweet taste
Of catching my face in the mirror.
The person I see is a fool.

Airplane

Airplanes drip red paint,
And blue and yellow and green
Drips fall from the sky,
Streaking rainbows as they glide.

Melancholy eyes,
I've always been afraid to die,
But somehow my heart doesn't quiver at the grave.
He's on a mountain, and I'm in a cave.
What makes this so insane?

Who here has heard of a sunny day?
When apples taste like the sour end of sweet May,
How could anyone deny the moment
When they kneel down to pray?
That's when faith meets Mars and the stars
And all the romances of far, far, and away.
Maybe I could catch his candy lips

Before he makes his escape.

In the dark, his arm drapes over me,
Eroding the next breath I take.
Is this what it's supposed to be?
For once, I have no shame.
What's it going to take?

For airplanes to burst through
The waking pain dripping paint,
Red paint
And yellow and green and blue,
I thought I'd do
What I wanna do,
But often what I ought to do
Remains unexplained.

His candy lips, my cluttered head,
A mat on the floor or a double bed—
I don't give a damn what evil says.

What evil has spoken,
What evil has torn tarnished, damaged, or broken—
I will count him as my token of my atonement.

Because I knocked,
And the door opened.

I step through,
Crouching down,
The Lord has me on my knees now.
Arms stretched out and receiving,
The clear sky I am seeing
Pours out paint

From an airplane,
My heart unstained
Because I received Grace.

For once, I stand still,
And I don't move to chase,
God sent a romance from far,
Far,
Away,

In an airplane,
Spreading color in my sky,
Melancholy eyes.
I take his hand when I pray;
I thank God for the one He sent my way.

Limbo

There's a pond I know about.
You can wiggle your toes in the mud.
The water is murky, conveying uncertainty.
Soot and sulfur surround it, calling my name from the brush.
Weak weeds waiver in the push and pull of the polluted air.
You find yourself someplace new,
It's called Nowhere.

If you shift your glance across the pond,
You can see faces in the trees,
Dodging from your peripheral vision.
They seize their sleep among the leaves.

Yet you don't sleep in Nowhere.
You couldn't if you tried.
The brown-blooded pit before you
Turns red before your eyes.

You couldn't believe it.
How could this be?
You wade in, until you're waist deep.
Obliviously, you tremble,
Mindlessly, you linger on—
You make your bed among the leaves

And wonder who that stranger is across the pond.

The Weather in November

It's in his steps;
I hear it in his voice.

The gentleness of fallen snowflakes that cannot yet stick to the ground.
They wander in the crisp morning air, melting on my dark oak hair.

Sinking into my scalp.

It's in his smirk;
It pours from his eyes

Like whiskey, like scotch, like sweet tea.
Making my knees weak.

He represents the wisdom one acquires
When they don't speak.

Just listen.

He's the man I never thought existed.
It weighs on his back but never falls from his lips.
The pain, the loss, the indifference.
Yet he dismisses hatred, evil, and bitterness.

He emits the warmth of a country church and the spark of citrus.
I pray my hand is in his when the end glistens
And if it isn't,

May I sense the fallen snow from a distance.

Pink

Dawn doesn't scream—
It trickles through the darkness,
Secretly swallowing the stars
And allowing rest for
The quite exhausted pink moon

Dusk, however,
Slugs the blue sky
With an orange array of lights,
Eventually sucking the last breath
Out of the evening's gentle caress.
With a bang, it moves on,
Beating like a drum,
Grabbing and snatching and scratching
The eyes out of the sun.

Yes,
The dusk drips blood.

Midnight zips up like a body bag,
Raging on with a vicious attack.
Ask him questions;
Beg for answers.
You will get none.
Oh, how the pink moon
Longs for the sun.

Nightmares drifting on the edge of reality,
Stone cold hands belonging to a pitiful personality.
Does the moon fade to grey in these hands?
Do the stars fall victim to a toxic romance?
And delicately dance on the tip of my nose,
They waltz preciously back to their pitch black home.

Waiting patiently in the east,
Softly fading away,
The dawn washes out all the gray.
The pink moon sinks into an ambient sleep.
Ominously, the dusk haunts the thoughts of childish dreams.

Until then,
I will have peace.

Straw Houses

**I stand with confidence
at the tip of a missile.**
At my side is paper and pencil.
The sights from up here are strikingly blissful.
I wish you could see it—
You built a house of straw, so I had to leave it.
I can't thrive as bones alone.
As you get closer, I get farther from home.
Couldn't you smell the sulfur?
Couldn't you smell the sewage?
I saw you holding your nose,
and as I tried to do it,
I grew faint.
God in heaven,
Get me out of this place.

Oh salty tears from heaven above,
Why have you cursed the souls I love?

Souls of sweet autumn, but their bodies are rancid.
I reap the harvest of the seeds I planted
And pray the ones I sewed in them take root,
But it was beyond any work that I could do.

Straw houses will fall,
Bitter cups will fail—
How could I bask in it all
With a life so frail?
How could I change my course,
Start anew
And leave you in the ignorance
You so frequently choose?
The painful reality is

I'm too strong to even go back for you.

Butterflies

I pet my hair in hopes it will feel like your hand.
Time spreads thin when you're away,
Thin and long like a never-ending thread.
I inch along,
God, art, and war.
Was it all wrong, was it all in vain?
I think too much when you're away.

Press into my skin like buttons on a rocket ship.
I want to be a mold for your muscles,
A shred of ribboned epidermis
To wrap around your fingertips.
Lick the corners of my lips,
Squeeze my bones into a citrus juice,
I move when you do.
I set a course for higher waters—
Count on me to be stronger when you falter.

My hands are open;
My hands are hopeful;
My hands bear weaknesses I reveal to you alone.
Take me broken;
Take me hopeful;
Take me into your home.

Welcome me to your safe spaces—
Abandoned innocence is contingent
Upon your growing independence.
My lover is my apprentice.
I will show you wonders galore,
But I pray you won't run once your feet hit the floor.

I cradle your wandering mind in my palms;
I hold it still for once.
It's been ramped for years, months, days—
I shake too much when you're away.
I hold you close to keep your thoughts at bay.
Have they ever let you rest?
Have they ever made a ruckus, then up and left?
Have they ever shattered your words into butterflies mid breath?
When I take your hand, I shoulder your stress,

And I'd never change it,
Even if these words
Should make me famous,
Even if our love is aimless,
Even if you broke down
My skeleton and rearranged it.

I will always be:
your evergreen

your poetry
your lightning streak
Your flying time
Your butterflies
Your angel wings.

The ice encrusting my aorta melts at the shine of your teeth.
May your rhythm restart my heartbeat.
My hands are starving;
My hands are hopeful;
My hands pray;

My hands grow quite weary when you're away.

Weeping Willow

Hold me down in the water,
Let the waves fill my lungs.
This was never just for fun.
You would let blood run
Before you would admit
That you're an egoist

Before you admit you're
Severely flawed.
You chew on my lip and eject
Your canine claws.
Oh, don't you love it when I fall?
Don't you love little—
Don't you love the empty words
You tell when you promised
You would meet me in the middle?

Don't you hate to fail, my love?
I hate it too,
But between my good habits and
Perfect weather, I'd let you lie to me forever.
Because I do it too.

The Man of God

I love the man that loves me.
Somehow he thinks highly of me.
It seems one of us has lied.

Although, he always tells the truth.
I am the one with the skewed moral compass,
And the mind that can't be trusted
But still he reminds me that God is what love is.

God is the foundation—there is no sin
That will break that relation.
The Father is worthy of our patience
Because he knows my soul
And has secured my salvation.

The man that loves me waits on God,
He savors the present because nothing is promised.
Sometimes his honesty clashes with my nonsense.

But it's perfect that way, he leads me closer to the cross.

My head is bowed in shame,
But he lifts it up so that I may praise,
So that we give thanks to the only righteous one,
The holy truth, and the only way.

The man that loves me prays devoutly;
The man that loves me doesn't doubt me;
The man that loves me follows the word,
not the world.

If we got what we deserved, we'd be on a cross,
But because of grace, we serve and save the lost.
The man that loves me, first, loves God.

So down that narrow path we walk,
We may have to crawl or run or simply be still.
Whichever it is, we will stumble on sin,
Reach great heights, fall on our faces,
Then continue the fight,
knowing we have already won.
I love the man that loves me,
for he is a man of God.

Chained

Where has my cigarette gone?

The ember moves closer to my fingertips,
The sting from the drag sizzling on my lips.
I huddle close to the smoke,
My head easing against the stench.

Where has my cigarette gone?
I had it in my hands.
The ash still on my pants,
I draw a second as my mind settles
Into a sore throat trance.

Where has my cigarette gone?
It's only been a minute—
Time stretched so tightly until the finish.
The butt blows off in the wind, and
I sing the blues.
The fourth goes quickly;
I feel the filter beneath my shoe.

Where has my cigarette gone?
This couldn't be my fifth.
My pack is looking weak versus
My never-ending kiss.
I suppose I should go inside;
My stomach's feeling sick.
The smoke break has come and went,
Though I know within the hour,
I'll be back again.

Three Steps from the Sun

Fear crackles and sparks up my body
Like electricity,
Like lightning striking at the top of my head,
I feel my limbs go dead.

My arms habitually reach for clarity,
They reach for something solid,
A tangible object,
A sparring sword,
A way out without having to speak anymore.

Did I mention that I'm tired?
Red delicious dread leaves me uninspired.
Can I get a pair of pliers to rip the wires from my jaw?
My feet don't lift at all,
Not even to fall or fetch or fly.

Let me know if you see my spirit draining from my eyes.
Call my name if my body miraculously moves from where I lie.
Get God on the phone if you see me hanging from a necktie.
Make my obituary the headline,
Black letters supersized
That read "heavy metal led to her demise."
Are you surprised?
You should be—

An early death could never catch me.
Press me down or stretch me,
One should know better than to test me.
I count my steps like they're my blessings;
I'll do better than what my best brings.

And in the morning when I wake,
I remind myself I'm more than my mistakes.
I'm more than laying in bed all day.
I'd like to say that I give more than what I take.
I won't be the one who breaks.
I'll calculate and come up with
The best way to survive my next day
And eat every last bite that's on my plate.
That's right, nothing goes to waste,

Not in these hands.
This sure as hell isn't how I planned it,
But it's what I got, so I can stand it.
In these hands, I hold a planet;
In this heart is where I command it;
In this head, I understand it.
And in my soul is where I've landed.

I'll always find a way back to me.
You may find a way to tackle me,
But I can haggle with uncertainty.
The price on life means the world to me.
I won't let it slip in vain.
I steady the course to ride the waves.

On the Fritz

I'll tell you a story, but I'll say this first:
I'm more than a wishbone and a pervert.
I'll tell you a tale, but I should disclaim:
I'm less than a cigarette butt and the turn of a page.

It all started in 6th grade where I was a dreamer,
12 years old with a mousey demeanor,

Too young to notice that the chatting of my enemies was quite beyond lucidity,
Knives and scissors became friends to me, and I couldn't recognize the oddity.

15 years old, and I was seeing nooses
In the hallways of my high school.
The chatter became louder,
And my dough brain became a cesspool.
18 was far too late to mitigate.

My mind went barreling off the rails of the interstate.
Smashing plates to kill the spiders,
Voices telling me my car was on fire,
Strange feelings that my head was full of wires,
Trying to outrun the static.
Hearing sirens and hiding under my mattress,
Every little noise bothered me.
I cut my body in search of technology.
I was on a fast track to a lobotomy.
There wasn't anything anyone could offer me
To keep me from acting obnoxiously.

Finally, I thought I got to be
Absolutely, unstoppably mad,
So I drove home to my mom and dad.
No judgment was passed,
Just an earnest desire to get help fast.

Twenty years old, I get diagnosed—
I begin seeing signs from long ago.
Back to twelve-year-old me,
Full of confusion and uncertainty.
A decade passed,
and if you can't do the math, that's twenty-two.
I've grown in wisdom yet remain confused.
Wise enough to recognize a screw is loose
But young enough to not know what to do.

Dead Flowers

Tulips of tobacco bloom in my lungs—
With a clock made of gold,
I watch my time run.
It dwindles little by little,
A knot forms in my throat,
First a choke, then a tickle.
My stomach is barren—
on my lips is a riddle.

True love was my first artwork,
My first nightmare, my first waste of time,
Abstruse as ten fingers intertwined,
So simple yet so complicated,
I was shocked to see how far we made it.
Every song I serenaded
Was stomped out and perforated.

I gave you a gift and said,
"Here, you can have this."
You let a glass heart slip
From your hands like plastic.
Our love was erratic,
Our love was dramatic,
Our love was toxic,
But it tasted fantastic.

Years have passed, but in my head, it's been days.
They tell me scotch tape also works for heartache.
But what about rhythm, what about the drums,
What about starting a fire just for fun?

Talk about bad advice.
I won't shoot a gun,
But I might throw a knife.
Tug on my arm, drag me to the soil,
Let me scrape at the dirt.
I don't think it's a matter of who left first.
What matters is all that was buried will be unearthed.
You will hear my name again, and when you do, I hope you cringe.
I hope you're riddled with regret,
Little by little, my Lady Macbeth.
This golden clock has ticked to an end.
May time finally stop when you rinse your hands.

Home Is Where the Heart Is

Hospital socks and crack rocks,
Dirty secrets in a shoebox
Left seizing on the sidewalk.
I look back on darker days.

Apprehensive, also earnest,
Black cars make me nervous.
I don't remember where I heard it,
But help is on the way.

May my mullet prevail over centuries.
By noon, I'm out of energy.
If I miss your arrival, send for me—
We can go to a quiet place.

Blood spills but with fair warning.
I skip breakfast every morning.
The pipe is hot, but I am boiling.
I travel through time in space.

The devil's clever, but I am faster.
His claws are dulled through
The sound of my laughter.
I am the ruler of fast food and dark matter.
May the sky leak tears on my face.

I tell you this home was never safe—

This home was never safe.

Champion

I feel younger than I did yesterday—
Maybe I'm aging backward.
There's a bounce in my step that I'm not quite used to yet;
There's a moment of private laughter and chocolate on my breath.

I'm dripping knowledge from my hands,
And I've finally caught the chance
Where I feel like dancing.
In what galaxy have I landed?
Tell me the planet I have commanded.
This is a world I don't recognize,
Wonder that I can't describe.

I am feeling paralyzed,
Not bedridden,
But such as a kitten
Is laying on my chest,

And I dare not move
To disturb her rest.
It's like I've found a lifeboat,
Laying back in the raft in a comfortable comatose.
For once, I don't feel the pull or throws.
The push, the wave,
I am gently washing the guilt away.

I feel all the solace of a lazy Saturday.
If you are, too, come to me,
Come with grace and effervescence—
I have no desire to be redirected.
I hope you can see it in my reflection
That remedy and tranquility are in my expression.

I feel my shoulders fall,
Not in a way that's disappointing
But in the measure of a new anointing.
This sensation deserves exploring.
I join the expedition with pride.
Finally, my bones begin to settle at night.
I've been made quiet but magnified
By all the loose ends I've been able to tie.

May my spirit be able to float—
It is no longer dense and lost
In rhythms and smoke.
I've found what makes life shimmer
Like a golden leaf of spring.
After all the harrowing.
I've silenced the beast.
In this moment, I know peace.

Lost on the Moon

Healthy, hearty, and hardly part of the party,

There's a gun in the couch and a green porch light on the house.
The glass gets passed around, and I watch the boys play their guitars.
The sucker on my right took five bars, and the girl on my left is heating a spoon.
Green smoke and empty folks fill the room.

Am I an outlier?

Do I belong in a world of dirty needles and
Backyard fires?
I tell myself this is the time of my life,
But I'm also a liar.
I'm also a cheat.
I've also caught a filthy disease

That binds my clanking bones
To the breeze and
Leaves me tapering in the trees,
Blended with the elements,
Creating space between my
Intentions and my intelligence.
With greed but also with elegance,
My existence proves to be irrelevant.

Why have I come here?
Has emptiness and an aversion
To pretension made me into the slime
That gets high with my reluctant permission?
Not to mention I never really had it.
No one wakes up one day and decides to be an addict.
At first, it seems like pretty sweet action
Until you climb out of bed and
You have one hell of a habit.

No distractions—
Time to clean up.
I disrupt
my moment
in
slow motion,
Off the couch,
"Where ya goin,"
I turn back but just for a moment.

"You guys are alright,
But I've lost my focus."

Winter Beach

Standing in the morphing sand,
Frigid wind and water sting my red hands,
Purple fingertips,
The sun's retreat leaves the elements
In a tangled and passionate interaction.

I exchange my excruciating brain for
Warm beer and aspirin
While the moonlight illuminates
My intrusive detachment.

Maybe I've been here before,
Not the place but the solemn headspace
That leaves something to be desired,
And though I admire the buttermilk fringe
On the bottomless blue ends of the wave's steady lapse,
I still suck in the wind
That twists up and bends like an early epitaph.

I've emerged from mishaps,
Havoc and bad habits,
Yet a bitter taste remains in my mouth from dissatisfaction.
I reconnect with my hollow chest
In the heatwave's absence.

I sing a slow song,
One about dying words and moving on,
One about accepting the worst and being wrong.
I tell the buzzards to move along
Because the poet in me is not yet gone.

Though it may seem like
I'm on the come down,
I'm slinking around,
Lying in wait for the pounce.

Bring these dying words to life:
I deny the worst and take a giant stride
Toward the finish line.
Open wide, they say,
So it goes, they say,
What do you know, they say,
She speaks in prose in the sober flow
Of the bottomless blue wave.

The Birth of October

The walls are painted white and gray.
There's a taste in my mouth that I can't escape—
It's pungent like trepidation.

After a slew of questions, I find myself under blankets,
Between thin sheets, Ambien dreams never leave me
forsaken.

I awake a revenant,
A force to be reckoned with,
A nurse that is less than benevolent
Calls my name to attend breakfast.

I fall in line
With faces that look like mine,
Bland as apathy, mapping its way through the mind,
Sour as the hours that cower in the shadow of time.
We share scars on our arms with a lack of pride.

In fact, we're ashamed
About how we ended up in this place.
Trading stories in the early morning
About drunken nights and our fall from grace.
We become family over weak coffee and cigarette breaks,

Yet my days are spent alone,
Even in utter lows and drawn-out poems.
My heart distends.
I feel no need to feign a pleasant countenance.
As the voices whisper, I surrender my sturdy defense.
I've become one with a plastic mattress.
Enormous pills hold me still in the thick of the madness.
They say lying becomes easy with practice,
So when my doctor asks me my status,

I say I'm doing fine,
Not depressed, not anxious,
No thoughts of suicide.
I don't tell him my sticky brain is fried
Or that I hear the wailing sirens at night,
Because if I did,
I'd never get out.
I keep the truth zipped up
Tightly inside of my mouth.

After that, I join the crowd.
Everyone's drawing or singing or settling down.
I crack open Bukowski to drown out the sound.
I've found solace in his words
And peace in the curse that this whole Earth suffers.
We've all lost our minds in one way or another.

Bukowski's Annoying

I no longer read Bukowski—
I find him childish and sappy,
Irritatingly unhappy and always nihilistic.

I no longer read Bukowski—
I think I've grown beyond him,
Always drunk and daunting.
I haven't found him profound—
Or mysterious or curiously genius,
As he so thinks of himself—
In a very long time.

Just because I read the Bible doesn't make me dogmatic or entitled.
In fact I'm desperate to be unbridled from my sin,
Desperate to be rescued from the idleness within.
Some say there is no God,

In fact, Bukowski said it a lot.
I used to think him charismatic,
When realistically, he was melodramatic,
Glorifying despair,
And crediting brooding as passion.
Over the years, he doesn't deliver
That same melancholy magic—
More like madness
Basking in filth,
Being passive.

All the poets choose the universe;
All the killers choose fate;
The scientists choose Mother Earth,
But there's no power in those names.
Their paths lead to pessimism and perpetual doubt.
Drown those voices out,
Lay your burdens down.
You have an opportunity worth exploring;
You will be new every morning.

Put your faith in The One Who Loves You
Because Bukowski is annoying.

The Starting Line

Thoughts can be fatal;
I try to reign them in,
But I am unable
Instead I play pretend
That my mental is stable.
To my chagrin,
I fall back in the pit,
Where my conscious is hateful.

Tenacity asks me to swing wide the door to possibilities.
I hike and climb and bike with faulty utilities.
Due to a lack of proper abilities,
I find that this journey is slowly killing me.

I am the one with broken bones.
Go ahead and stone the sinner,
Hurl your rocks til I wither.
I am vacant,

Impatient,
Emotionally ancient,
But never a quitter—
Ask me again if I'm bitter.
I extract splinter after splinter,
As I watch my heart gain weight
And my body get thinner.
I'm merely playing to not lose
Instead of reigning as victor.

I surrender to the chatter as I lie down;
I awake in the morning with their words on my mouth.
All ten of my fingers clinch onto doubt as
I shout out proudly that I'm a sick fuck,
A sitting duck, and lost in the rapture.
I've set camp in disaster
And every second thereafter
Is a test of wits and physical power.
Hold on tight because this carnival ride
Just gets faster and faster.
I don't care how far I go—
I just pray that it matters,

And I'll give it a week before I stumble,
yet defend my honor.
I'm late for a date with the Holy Father;
I unbutton my shirt as I await my slaughter,
Because the deeper you get,
The hotter and hotter

I puff out my chest because I play to win,
And if you were to ask me again if I am bitter,
I'll repeat the tale of when I was a beginner.

KIDS

Little plastic
Little flame
Little glass
Little blade

Little cuts
Going nuts
The afterthought is pain

Big mistake
Big and bad
Little whispers
Going mad

Stop and go
Heavy flow
Scarlet red
No one knows

I wipe away the pain

CREEPERS

Coated in liquid black static,
They appear around corners
And hide in the attic—
A dark fuzz,
A stretch and a snap,
A sinister presence,
A steady tap.
They stand quite still,
Or they move with haste—
I looked one dead in the eyes,
But he had no face.
I'd imagine that they sting to the touch,
But I've never gotten close enough.
I never even tried to run.
They know how to find me;
They morph through the walls
With perfect timing.
They know I can see them;
They know of my dread—
My fear is that they're back again.

Big City Dreams

I stumble out of the driver's seat—
My sneakers hit the pavement
Harder than a broken dream.
I swing wide the door to
A kingdom called Valero,
To which the cracked tile
Is its peasants, and I am the pharaoh.

A bottle of mad dog sings my name,
The clerk behind the glass asks me my age.
I say I'm twenty-one with dying lungs and a baby face.
He takes my word and stores my change.

I bounce out to the curb to smell the gasoline.
This city breathes catastrophe,
And I am one of its many sheep.
There's sin in our homes and trash in our streets;
There's strays in our yards,

Dents in our cars, and bugs in our sheets;
There's nothing left that bothers me.
This city taught me monotony,
What it's like to live on botany lane.
My neighbor serves me drugs on the windowpane,
Dying young with the world to gain.
Who says I have to live with shame?

I am one with the herd.

Idle Hands

Bad news paired with old shoes makes for a rainy day.
I've got $5 in my pocket, and I'm sure I'll let it go to waste.

It's an ugly morning,
The kind that thins out the sun's embrace,
But in the concrete swamp of Houston,
The weather remains in disarray.

My thoughts are out of place.
They seemed to have gone missing,
Whistling through the vents,
And wrapping around my ceiling fan,
Ultimately losing my attention.

I'm faced with subtle apprehension.
It weaves its way into my shirt and up my neck;
It hangs around doorknobs and leaks from my shower head.

Today I don't feel like talking—
I have no sense of belonging.
I find it hard to steady my pace.
I spill the contents of my brain
Onto paper.
It stains and steams vapor
Up into the heavy clouds.

I marinate in distasteful doubt,
The kind that makes me nauseous.
I know my doom awaits me,
So I peel back the lid to my coffin.

I bathe in the silk so comfortably,
Thinking this world has had enough of me,
But I know better than to glorify death.
I climb out of my unending rest
And lift the haze that coats my days
In existential dread and slow breaths.

The $5 in my pocket sings a song to me
About a strong and creamy cup of coffee,
So I slip into a denim jacket and slink
To the diner across the street from me—
At least I have consistency.

S104

I feel a presence behind me,
A looming beast
Casting its shadow over me,
Disturbing the peace—
My peace—
Existing ever so silently.

My sight stings so vibrantly.
The lights are undeniably
Too bright in here.

Everyone seems so at peace,
Their peace
Existing ever so righteously.

I smell their coffee,
Their caffeinated liquid inspiration;
I overhear their conversations,

Their ambitions unabated,
While my foundation lacks stability.

Nonetheless,
I brilliantly
Stand among them

As someone who's overcome tribulations,
Exceeded expectations, and been wildly underestimated,

Yet still I am intimidated
By the unpredictable crowd.
I twist my head over my shoulder
To pair an entity with the sounds,
The noises so complex,
I guess the vortex that exists behind my forehead
Makes me believe I can't achieve greater things
As the ones that stand among me.

So brilliantly,

I have to work resiliently—
Three times,
Four times,

Five times as hard as them
To ever be a part of them.

Not to be mistaken,
My ambitions are unabated.
I'll shoot for the stars and land,
Three times,
Four times,
Five times as far—

My brain speaks the language of bizarre,
But I'll weather the lunacy as long as I have the opportunity
To win the battles of my heart,

The looming beast can starve.
He will not feast on this day.
I have far too many things to do
To let him slow my pace,
And the ones who stand among me
Will not recognize my fear,
For I have conquered many giants
Just to be standing here.

Red Bumps

Red bumps, red bumps,
They appear when I wake up.
Warm milk, moonlight drips
From the night sky onto
My bitter wine-colored bed.
My claws eject and carry me
Knee deep through sudden death.
Few words escape my shivering breath,
"Red bumps red bumps"
They rise up, I writhe up.
Fear pools at my feet
Like a mudslide running over me,
My senses perceive erroneously.
At the break of day, the red bumps go away.
No proof left,
Except the scrapes on my legs,
My stomach gargles relief and rage,
Hoping to never again have to face
The rash that yields no escape.

You won't hear me speak of

The red bumps, red bumps.

Rainbow Motion

Imagine:
A heart that beats to the music
Of helium highs and stark winter nights

Picture:
The taste of lemon lime
And the scent of fresh cream
I am searching

For arms that reach many moons
And retrieve stardust
From planets around the sun,
Forevermore,
A stronger reflection of the person
I have become—

Someone who understands forgiveness
And knows that grace is a walk toward redemption.
I will be uplifted
By the sound of their smile and the taste of their kisses;
I will be defended
By their desire to provide protection.
A holy infection of an honest connection
That can turn forest fires into amity.
A rock hard and pure heart insanity
That inspires me to achieve all I plan to be.

Humanity
Will stagger at a bond so fully blessed
We will be a lover's envy, a sailor's silk sea,
And a child's nest.

You can find me here—
All you have to do is wait for our time, dear,
Because I have set the table for two,
And every stride that I take
Is on a journey toward you.

Jelly Brains

Jelly brains have me fading,
Slipping off into black
Cloaked in the aftermath
Of mixed medications
I watch the clouds bask
In the sun's meditation.
In the easy sting of its golden rays,
I could never relax in the same way
Beneath its yellow wave.

I pace quietly in an empty house—
I've lost my mind in the folds of the couch.
I watched it slip down,
Swallowed up by the fabric.
I spark my third square from a
Cheap pack of Mavericks.
Hoping to draw my thoughts
From the labyrinth that lives in my head,

I slither under my bed,
Heavy hearted,
My eyes have darkened,
Spirit and body departed,
My lungs are lethargic.
My breath is depleting—
I check to see if my heart is still beating.

I close my eyes,
Pull in oxygen,
Or arsenic in disguise,
I aimlessly wander,
Feeling less than alive
But more than dead.

I live in limbo where the bats are blood red,
And the vultures can sing.
They soar through acid rain in the spring.
Honey drips in the winter,
The trees give you splinters,
And the devil has wings.

I stare at the ceiling
And pop my pills.
The ants trek across the windowsill;
They trickle over my hands and onto my face.
I slip back into the dazed state,
Desperately trying to navigate
The thick fog, the sleepy haze,

The daylight steals my heart away,
Making me weak.
The twilight brings tears that leak
Over my cheeks and onto my neck;
I hold my palm to my chest,

Dreading my next step,
Loathing the morning to come,
The break of day—
I plunge backward into jelly brains.

ROCK BOTTOM BLUES

The predator stands
At the edge of my bed.
I open my legs.
The white power glimmers
In lines I erase
As I lower my face,
So much to be said.

I silence it all
With a hash pipe
In a bathroom stall,
I brush my teeth with alcohol.
I start the morning
with three shots of fireball—
I'm wired wrong,
I've tried to give this shit up,
but it's protocol.

I shut their mouths when I give it up or put it out,
My stomach growls throughout this heavy drought.
There's cracks in the ground, yet I go for another ring
Around this roundabout,

A self-fulfilling prophecy.
I don't feel like myself
Without a bloody nose or an STD.
My friends find it funny,
As if it's a thrill to live like a junkie,

Yet they tell me to proceed with caution.
If I keep my foot on the gas, I'll end up in a coffin;
I've got to admit that I'm numb way too often;
I am no longer quick witted, my body is rotten.

I am disheartened
To say the least,
Haste the day
That I make my peace
And act full grown,
Learn how to be alone
Without getting drunk,
Or high, or downright stoned.

It's time to start acting right:

Find out how to be content
Without getting laid every night.
There's shame in this life
To hang your head out the window
And puke at stop signs,
To pass out on the asphalt
Underneath the streetlights,

Cops banging on my door
Two hours past midnight,
Waking up with a stranger
And a nicotine appetite,
Laying cross eyed, poolside,
Nine beers on a weeknight.

Took me five years to realize
I'm not bulletproof,
Having LSD dreams beneath my parents' roof,
Barred out on the carpet with piss in my shoes—
It's time for a breakthrough.
Enough of the sex addiction and substance abuse,
This self-sabotage will have my head in a noose.
I open my eyes to see the life I could lose,

Or maybe I'm just stuck in the rock bottom blues.

RECOVERY

Healing is the hardest part,
Bandaging blisters that have festered
Far too long to be recognized as the
Slash wounds they once were—
They've woven together,
Leaving scars that serve as a reminder
Of the hardened heart
That I harbored and sat like a heavy stone
In the armpits of the forest.

Forgotten and stranded,
My lips turning blue from romances,
Followed by abandonment,
Shivers delivered to the depths of my chest
From desperately trying to tie up loose ends.
Steps in the right direction means sacrificing
the sins that hogged my attention.

Palms facing the sky,
I allow my eyes to gaze
Upon the deceit
I so ruthlessly repeated.
I've torn every heart
That's ever needed me,
Seemingly without a doubt.

With humility, I turn around
And recognize the damage I've done,
The battles I've lost, and the love I have won.
I honor the ones that remained,
The arms that never picked apart my shame
And forgave the decisions
That stained down to my bones.

I uphold a new standard
Of standing on my own two feet,
Without bulldozing my time to come.
Forgiveness and grace meet halfway
To spark a bond that cannot break,
And I bring justice to the table
As someone who's been hollowed
And mistaken and is now awakening
To the sound of a crushing stone
In the armpits of the forest.

Remember No More

Bring me to a tundra of tomorrows,
High peaks and hills to borrow,
And bring me back to the books
I have stacked in the closet,
Pay no mind to what caused it.
I am awaiting the creation of a path
That leaves me shaking,
Like the dwindling leaves of autumn—
Pay no mind to what brought them,
Just take in their patience,
The awe-inspiring greatness
Of a chilling November.

Bring me to a typhoon of laughter,
Moments spent in a winding pasture,
Where I disregard spreading disaster
And lie down in peace—
I want a thick fog rolling over me,

Not one of uncertainties but one of warm tea
and the scent of a library.
Carry me across rivers that
Spark the sharing of memories
And forgiving enemies—
I've always had an affinity
For innocence,
So take me to a forest of dependence,
Where leaning in
On the trees and twigs
Brings comfort to a heart that listens.

I stretch out my tendons as the clamor of my skeleton in the heat of the desert reveals the intentions behind my endeavors.
Take me to the forgotten fields that define forever and leave me there to take in the air and bind my bare feet and the grass together.

Pay no mind to the weather.
Forget the aging of my skin—
Pay no mind to the distance
From myself and my afflictions,
I am far beyond giving attention
To the shadows that exist in fiction.
I am rising from a tundra of tomorrows
And leaving sorrows in the moments they occurred.
Beyond that, I move onward.

Betrayed by the Senses

My hands look scaly in the Houston rain,
Despite the forecast, the sky is ominous today.
I stand in the parking lot and look both ways,
All I can feel is the wind in my face.
The sweat on my palms,
The ringing in my ears has gone on for too long,
And the colors keep getting brighter.
The cars sound like planes, and the clouds are on fire,
My eyes are tired.

My breath plummets to my stomach,
My heart drops to my feet,
I smell blood in the street.
The voices rhyme to the beat,
The steady beat, the static hum
Of that Houston rain.

I feel the drum
In my chest,
The sweat
On my neck,
And every push
And pull of my
Nicotine breath
Brings me closer
To the kiss of death.
I spiral down and press
My fingers into my ears,
The sounds I hear
Taste stranger than I feel.

I shuffle into a building and collapse into a chair,
Before I know it, my best friend is there.
He's taking me to a familiar place.
I try hard to recognize stimuli,
But my mind goes blank
. . .
I had to go home from work that day.

All These Words

All these words,
They rush through my hands,
Like a fierce current,
My fervent
Desire for a great escape
Turns to calamity,
Coursing quickly,
Crushing sanity.

All these words
Racing past my ears
And flowing through my chest,
Increasing my heartbeat,
I tremble and sweat.
They spin violently around me,
Their ferocious noise
Never fails to astound me.

All these words,
They pump like a bass
Dumb and snap like a snare,
I plunge my head through the
Mylar to escape their stares,
And I swear,
To fight tooth and nail,
To crawl through the flames,
But I crumble when they say my name.

All these words,
My sprints can't match their speed,
I'm left wounded by their feral teeth,
My voice can't match their sound—
They're loud,
Pulsing like a beating heart
And rattling my skull,
Like the cage of a gnarly beast.
Go ahead and eat—
You'll find no meat.
I'm skin and bone,
And I'm never alone,
The voices keep me company,
So be sure to go slow
And speak up to me.

All these words,
They move gracefully,
Yet sting viciously,
Like the hasty bite of a viper,
Like the agile bullet of a sniper,
I fight her,
But the fruits of the siren
Just keep getting riper.

She sends the voices
To the back of my head,
Where they reverberate
And just come back again.

All these words,
What will it take to rid them?
They may stay forever,
Damned to relive them.

All these words roar the loudest
When I'm ready to sleep.
I'll wake the next day,
Damned to repeat.

Man Down

It's hard to know if they're the aliens,
or if the alien is me.
I look to the Houston skyline—
It seems all-knowing.
In the haze, I am one with the moonlight,
Somehow the cracks in the concrete
Are morphing beneath my feet.
I huddle closer to the heat of the buildings.
I don't know if the visions are beatable—
It's treatable.
Will I ever defeat the noise?
Maybe if I wasn't me,
The weakness is relief.
It's easier to seek warmth
In the comfort of my sheets
Than it is to strain to see a light
That I can never reach—
The warrior is me.

The wind lets out a chill,
Breathing together with the sirens,
The gunshots, the bleeding,
The ongoing need to stifle
The tedious tasks of a life so bleak.
Maybe it's me.
The sun lets out a shriek.

It's morning.

No Rest

I feel like a foreigner in my own bed.
Why should the trees against the daylight pose a threat?

Why should I stand still?
My feet on the ground move in a heartless drag.

I hear the hum from the pounding in my chest,
No time to rest,
No need to—
I have to find a mask I can breathe through.
The expense of my grin is suffocation,
Out from my mouth flows meaningless statements.

I've switched places with a different dimension,
I close my mouth to avoid the attention
I get from the friction in my subtle behaviors.
They ask what it's like to waver.

I tell them I'm a giver among billions of takers who move in unison toward trends and religious saviors.

I float aimlessly amidst the galaxies,
There's no variation between fiction and reality.
How could it be that my internal chemistry is that of a different entity?
My world is filled with enemies—they surround my immediate vicinity,
They stand outside my door,

They watch from afar.
When I catch them looking,
I can't let them know I know who they are.

The glitches in my brain
Shake me awake from a restless sleep,
They pull at my feet,
They bang at the door, they peak through the blinds,
There is no rest for the tireless mind,
No time to rest,
No need to,
I have to find a lens I can see through.
The cost of my spark is a vapid gaze,
Cloaked in bullets I feel no pain,
Shot through the bone and into my engine,
I truck along with no good intentions,
Just hopelessly descend into my opposite dimension.

Yes, I'm there again,
Patiently awaiting my ascent into heaven.
Too bad my sins are heavy enough to drown in,

But here it comes,
The next wave, the next bad break,
The wreckage in my closet,
Spilling into my food, my drink, my sex,
My sleep, my rocket ship chapped lips,
My cracked glasses, and life I hardly live.

I read the next words off my script;
I question whether I really exist;
I sit alone and stare into the dark soul of the earth.
It gobbles me up into its deep bottomless stomach.
I rot in the center of the fiery core,
Wondering when the stranger sitting on my bed
Will come to my rescue.

Under My Skin

They're in the crowds,
Floods of hot bodies clanking together
To create an unsanitary mound of discomfort.

Within the mix, there's the creepers,
The watchers,
The ones that stare.
They cloak me with anxious sweats;
They well my eyes with the tears of innate fear,
Tears of familiar terror.

I can't leave my house without
The pounding in my temples,
The heavy weight of my own hands,
Dragging me to the concrete with loneliness,
With indignant agony
While apathy floods the vapid crowd around me.

The surge of human life that continues to bump along,
Like cattle like a half-sung song,
Without noticing the empty eyes that corner me,
Ignoring me.
How come the world swirls around me
While I am suffering a catatonic standstill?

Take a pill—
This should make it better;
Breathe easy—
This will calm your mind,
But the black pit in the night sky
Still lurks behind me.
The lithium
Only gives them
A chance to come find me.

Keep your head down, keep your head down,
They're emerging through the vicious
Crowd now.
Everyone thinks they found out
Something I don't know about.
I swear I'm not crazy,
Still they take me
To a professional with a fancy diagnosis.
Don't say I have psychosis.
I know this feeling,
The trembling, the shivering,
The unmitigated shock,
While you stand around with your stopwatch,
Waiting for me to pop.

The fog rolls over the crowd,
Their faces stand out.

Heavy air sits upon their shoulders,
But not holding them to the earth
My feet are grounded in the dirt.
Heaven and hell couldn't move me,
Fear maps its way through me.
The sobbing sky molds them into
The ominous monstrosity that haunts me.
Death alone is daunting.

The escape is clear, but I plead out of sheer desperation
That I'm spared from the aching heart, the intimidation.
If I get the slightest inclination
Of the skeletons behind me,
They peak from the corners to find me.
I hide away,
Conceal my face,
And pray to God that they don't recognize me.

Calypso

Born into beauty,
Baby, you're glorious,
This is all new to me.
You're the vine that
Wraps around my legs—
I'm notorious for red wine,
So let me bear your grapes.

I'm aching for a taste,
Grant me a sip of your kisses,
Let me bring you to my lips,
You pass over my tongue like silk and citrus.

Your gentleness is innate;
Your effervescence is captivating.
How could I ever surprise you?
I push myself into your rolling hills,
But I don't think I can survive you.

You have me in a whirlpool,
I am going in no direction,
I am searching for a seraph,
Her voice is a compelling confession.

Her eyes are grey but warming,
Like a silver flame on a burning tree.
It's December in her heart,
But I'm increasing in degrees.
She's ravishing to me—

A stolen tiger lily,
She's every word of the Bible,
She's a bounding soliloquy,
She speaks to me,
And to no one else.

I'm chained to her empty church,
Her ringing bells,
Yet I am content with slavery—
She is the one who is holding me.
Take your swords and run,
There is no defeating her majesty,

Yet there's a nightmare in her eyes,
A form of torture that I can't describe.
She's the cold wind in the morning breeze,
The kiss of death that comes to life.

She's the mural that I'll never be;
She's the poem that I can never write;
She pours sweet serendipity into me
And cloaks the sky in the black cape of the afterlife.

Turn me into dust,
Spread me over the Earth's surface,
Baby, you fly beyond this planet,
You are the galaxy, and I'm the Grand Canyon.

There are beauties about you
That I can't imagine.
I climb the highest mountains
to feel your touch.

I fall like an avalanche;
I am the filthiest mudslide;
I reach and conquer such great heights,
But I reap the consequences of greed.

Now, what is it that you think of me?
I wave my white flag in defeat,
I will always crave your energy,
The anger in you swallows me—
Spoken like a true rebel.

I'm within earshot of the devil,
But I drew the landscape for the heavens,
You scrape your way to dead ends,
The blood thickens
And you mock the fear within me,
You take up arms against me.

Where I thought you were glorious;
You were horrific.
I drank poison when I tasted citrus,
And instead of gentleness, there was trickery,
You made a fool of me,
A dying soliloquy.

You may have sounded like a siren,
But the songs were vapid screams.

I know you now, calypso.
You'll never conquer me.
I'd rather stand alone than
Die enamored by a serpentine.

I am firm as the earth,
I'll pass on like the river over stones,
You're nothing but a water witch,
Swept off in the undertow.

Whenever You Don't See Me Looking

She doesn't have to speak to be poetic

Because it comes from her smile—
Her harlequin eyes hold my hands
Tighter than her teeth on my lips.
I'd collect the brightest stars
To give her in the palm of my hand.
She makes me feel that big;
She makes me taste the little things
And shows me the universe
When I kiss her cheek;
She makes me feel holy.
The whole world breathes
With her—
She doesn't ever walk alone,
For the leaves fall behind her;
She could ride backwards
Into the pits of Texas
And the moon will find her,
Peaking through the windows

and taking the rain from her hair
so the sky can cry vanilla tears.
Every devil on my chest
Melts with her laugh,
And every scrape
On my back from
Hitting rock bottom rougher
Than the Columbia rocket to water
Feels romantic beneath her fingerprints.
Believe me when I say she's perfectly flawed,
Well-guarded but recklessly follows her heart,
Recklessly follows roads to nowhere
When she is the wildest adventure I know,
And there is no
Way that God is not an artist
When that smile's on her face,
The whole planet falls in love
With the way she chases fate,
And every day my world grows with me,
I'm a tiger, she's Aphrodite.
God made her with wings,
But He was afraid she'd blind me,
Bright like the sun but glows like a candle,
She can be dimmed only by gentle romanticism,
Blooms like an aster in autumn,
Like lilac in the spring,
She drapes her wit across my shoulders
And leaks charisma with every step,
Puts angels to shame with the words on her breath
I've gone insane with sweet heartache,
I'm a red-ribboned basket case.
She is lost somewhere in her mind,
And only the moon and I
Are crazy enough to find her.

THE LION OF JUDAH

I am no Christ figure—
There is not a heart beating in me,
Just a fractured and haggard frame
That is far too frail for my age,
Crusted in skin that is too pale for my taste,
Cloaked in a thick fur made for winter,
But the summer's heat has me pinned to a cross.

There are worlds I've built for just one woman,
Parts of me that didn't exist previously.
Love is a stale flavor of toxic waste or wasted beauty;
Love is what I chased when there was no way my worlds
Could satisfy the appetite of the black hole in her brain.

The Lord reveals all my reasons for wanting something
Love has proved to be the ultimate form of taxidermy
Ripping out my insides to stuff me with vapid ambition
And unspoken discontentment.

Is there something I'm missing?

Could my modest 26 letters capture the stench of my heart
Rotting from a mix between STDs and gangrene?
And I almost forgot the fever that starts when I count her steps,
When she walks while my own legs collapse beneath me.

She wanted my skeleton,
When all I could offer was
My heartbeat

I am heir to the throne of punk rock and shark teeth—
Could she miss the hands that played guitar too loudly,
That pulled a molded shower curtain around me,
That heated my wet bones over a gas stove?

There is a fractured and haggard frame
That is far too pale for a handsome face,
That is drenched in bleach in an attempt
To reverse the way the past stains.

The way she tasted on a Thursday, you could say,
I was betrayed with a kiss—
You could say my disease-ridden and overly intimate
Heart might've been worth more than thirty silver pieces.

You could say
That I am too romantic
And idealistic for reality,
As if that could somehow
Loosen her undisputed
Grasp on me.

She is a perfectly crafted masterpiece
That very temporarily fell for,
A fifty-cent ball cap at a dollar store.
My gentle disposition and one-track mind
Couldn't hold her attention,
The stars in her own eyes are bigger
Than the ones that I could give.

I would tear the moon from the sky,
But for now, I'll just howl until
It lands at my feet—
I'll push wind through my lips
Instead of her breath that has now
Blessed another lover's cheek.
And the thorns in my scalp produce
The blood that won't allow me to see,
It's like a spear in my side,
Like I have to heave
My entire body upward to breathe
As the crowd is shouting "Crucify!"

There once was a betrayer and a sacrifice,
A sinner and a bowie knife,
A fractured frame and a masterpiece,
Twenty-six letters and wasted beauty.

The Living, the Liars, and the Lifeless

Burn,
For silent sensitivity,
I've been angry, but I don't bend,
They see the cross around my neck
But missed the sin upon my lips,
And I move quickly,
I sprint enough to run completely out of breath.
If death is near come nearer—
I am here but I can't hear.
I'm either faint of heart or slightly deaf of ear.
I begin
Again for the title's sake.
Are there weights
On my tongue
That make my words drag on?
Are there sharks inside my body
That carry guns and launch bombs?

I am no greater than my inequities, but I am
Sharper than the pain in my chest,
Bolder than my silent sensitivity, though
All my luck is stolen, all my faith is borrowed,
I am a wrist with many blemishes
And a head that's harshly hallowed.
If the ocean sunk itself in the deep,
Would I still be here tomorrow?

Burn,
For silent sensitivity.
I'm not angry, I am bent,
There is a cross around my neck
But only truth upon my lips,
And I move slowly,
Tiptoe enough to even silence death.
If he should be near,
I will not fear his touch,
But I will
Hear
His steps.

Road to No Place in Particular

The wind hums and bumps into us,
I speak against your lips,
My bitter coffee breath
Passes over your tongue.

The wind hums and runs through our fingers,
Clumsily tumbles and fumbles for a dream,
Singing lullabies off key.
He wraps us up in trash from the streets
Because the smell keeps us awake.

Pasting newspaper over our faces,
But we still fail to see the world around us.
Nothing makes sense besides the steam
From the shower that carries out my laments.
Nothing can open me,
Save your wandering hands beneath bedsheets;
Nothing is bright,

Except for the tall glass of liquid black victory
You give to me when I am lonely.

They buried me long after
The days where I was dead,
Buzzards ran off with my teeth,
That's why I stopped eating.
My coffin was built out of rotten wood,
And the lies that I kept thinking about
And telling myself.

Then the wind would hum and cough up magic,
You came to me like a pestilence of forgotten passion,
I grew tiger stripes and roared from the basement
At the broken blinds, crowded sidewalks and lamp lights.
You smiled at my devotion,
Played with fire, wore black,
Encouraged sudden death,
Heart attacks, and overdosing.
Default emotion was hate,
Drank blood for the taste,
I cried often and scraped my body
On the pavement that led to my
Unknown destination.
I cut my hair and covered my face,
Wore flannels with torn up shoes
And called it style.

Baby, if you love me, you're a necrophile;
Darling, if you love me, you're a liar;
My dear, if you love me, you're on a fast track
To flashbacks, regrets, havoc, and dissatisfaction,
But I'd self-destruct in your absence,

So keep me close, and
I won't wander,
I'll fawn over and ponder
All the curls and curves and cures you carry
For each one of my dying words.
I'll lead you into sewers and caves and up staircases
And into toxic waste,
Up to the roof, into the water,
Into the Earth's core,
Onto the moon,
Into the sky,
Under covers
And behind my eyes,
Just to teach you that our love
Will kill before it dies—
Our love will kill before it leaves us.

I am gentle snow coating Sunday morning,
You are dynamite rolling through a church building;
I am untied Chuck Taylor's.
You are an electrical wire stuffed down a sink—
You're the hail that's falling over me.
Reign over me, let me be a witness to your elegance
And everything you're thinking.
After you, writing became easy.

After a while, I'm pulling fast food from the trash cans
And standing on my toes to kiss you.
You're making mean jokes and rolling your eyes,
You've painted yourself onto my aorta
And nosedived into my bloodstream.
I could never be rid of you
Or chew through this connection.
We've coughed up blood,

Ran into demons, and bumped into God,
Sucked up all the wind until the air is still. Still. Still.

Your iris leaks perfection,
We're dripping wet on the carpet
That's already stained by adolescent recklessness.
You'll fall asleep in my arms tonight,
And in the morning, we'll plow through the galaxy
And sputter coffee from the holes in our bodies,

But for now,
I'll cover you in silk I stole from heaven,
Give you jewels and human bones.
I'll speak against
Your lips and pass poetry
Over your
Tongue.

Thought Flood

I'm a firm believer in the fact
That everyone's a hypocrite,
And just because you say something
Doesn't mean that you meant it.
I also think hate's a lot like spit—
Once you let it go,
It's not long before you feel it
In your mouth again,
And love's a lot like teeth when you lose it,
Replacing it won't be the same.

This is a confession,
Maybe more of a thought flood,
Pushing to the ends and edges
Of the earth,
Swallowing up the ground beneath your feet,
And I know you don't think much of me
But hear me out—

Yes,
Hear me out.
You slash and spike
With swords of doubt,
Stabbing into the purity
Of the finest beings of humanity
Fighting for equality,
Yet insist on being a supremacy.

I can't tell if this is ironically hilarious
Or a contradicting pain in the ass,
But let me tell you this . . .

It's hard to give unless you're asked.
Maybe that's why you all run in circles,
Trying not to step on one another's toes,
But behind the scenes, you trample across
Each other's feet, rat racing toward
What you think is a new beginning.

You applaud your simple mind
When you think you hit fast forward,
But you really pressed rewind.

Let me take a different approach—

I'll tell you the *do*s instead of the don'ts

1. Find joy in the little things.
2. If you hate it, hit the road.
3. Love. Because it matters.
4. Don't assume what you don't know.

Be willing to take apart the pieces and rebuild the weaker spots,
Realize life as you live it and NEVER try to be something that you're not.

This is a thought flood of a writer and a believer,
A robot, a hot shot, a rotting corpse, and an over thinker.

Take me seriously because I begged you to hear me out

Listen to a thought flood of a thinker who stopped refusing to think out loud.

THE CALLING

I went through hell,
Lately I feel like
I never returned.
You beckon me back
With genuine concern,

Yet what I've learned:
All the things I think I know
Turned me wretched,
Left me scorched and alone;

All my rules,
What I knew,
Is worth nothing
Compared to following You.

———

Child, I know all the truth,
Back when no one else
Could get it through to you.
You thought of me;
You always knew
Who you ought to be,
Your heart is written
Into prophecies.
You're my creation—
Your name is melded in the stars.
They shine to show you who I am
So you may believe in who you are.
When you're away from that smoke
That thickened the air,
That city that made you so scared,
You can see them in my clear violet midnight.
Child, I will be standing there,
Beckoning you,
Rescuing you,
It hurts to see you destitute.
Child, I've protected you,

All the wicked things you know:
The skin you burnt,
The glass in your toes,
All the horror that evil made known,
Shrouded your shoulders,
Roots on your throat.

My Son was right beside you,
Guarding your soul.

———

Father, You're my destiny,
The devil made a mess of me,
Yet You are the Redeemer,
You made a double-edged schemer, a believer.
Lord, I look to You,
In this life there is no other truth
Than the words from Your breath,
Released to the earth when You lifted the dead
And revealed the good news.
The gospel is alive in me,
Every word I write will be
To Your glory—
I'll tell Your story.
Everyplace my foot falls,
From this day forward,
I come at Your call.

Katie Giletto is a born and raised Texan with a unique mix of a somewhat crass, fervently spiritual, and excitedly upbeat personality. Her journey through addiction, rock bottoms, and recovery, and her ongoing battle with schizophrenia, have shaped her life and her poetry.

Strange Places includes select poems spanning from her teenage years to her current life. Now in her mid-twenties, Giletto offers a style of untamed and raw poetry that is strikingly authentic and personal.

Through sharing her work, she intends to comfort the lost and rejoice with the found.

Connect with Giletto and read more of her work at
KatiesPoetryPlanet.buzz.

Made in the USA
Columbia, SC
30 January 2023